Unvarnished Truths

Sophia Desiatov

Presentation by *BookLeaf Publishing*

Web: www.bookleafpub.com

E-mail: info@bookleafpub.com

ISBN: 9789395756747

First edition 2022

DEDICATION

To my family and friends who have been a fountain of support and love.

And to the younger me, who thought this would not be possible:

'Everything in life is writable about if you have the outgoing guts to do it, and the imagination to improvise. The worst enemy to creativity is self-doubt' - Sylvia Plath

Part 1: The Voiceless

Apples and Mirrors

She gave me midnight hair, snow white skin and blood-red lips, but she didn't give me a voice, only the tune of a nightingale that would entrance any man who would hear. They call me the fairest in the land, but don't they know what a curse they place on me? I was shackled before I was born, moulded by a mother's wish, created by a vain desire to have something more beautiful than her. I was damned then, only to live as someone's Muse, only to be seen and touched, but not heard, because who would want to hear me when they can gaze at my beauty? Mirrors tell me I am fair and sweet, like an apple, but how shallow are the ripples of glass! They do not see how I feel, how I long to run like the deer in the forest, free and wild. Do they not know that beauty does not last, that it will wither and rot until nothing is left but a husk? Oh, how I wish my hair was black like ash, skin as white as a corpse, lips as red as clay, for then I wouldn't be seen with lustful eyes, touched with wandering hands and lips that would take my virtue away on a coffin-bed. Doesn't she know that I did not ask for this, that I would wish away my beauty if I could, gift it to her inside a lead chest if that is what it took to make her jealousy flee? I would scar myself until I was as hideous as Medusa, so that any man would turn into stone or flee from my monstrous face. I would scream and rage at the world if I could, but I must become like a statue, beautiful and mute, waiting for my prince to come.

Ashes

Be brave and kind and generous, you said as you brushed my golden hair with soft strokes. You must always be kind. I thought that was the wisest thing you had ever said, but I didn't realise that it was a chain to keep me tethered. Too late, I didn't ask the question. Why must I be brave and kind and generous to them that push me into the cinders, slap me in the face when I don't have breakfast ready for them? Why must I smile as red blossoms on my cheek like a rose, or when my fingers turn black with ash and my agony? I only wanted to be free, like the majestic eagle that soars above the ground, unrestrained, wild. And yet I am the lone canary, compelled to sing a tune or face the wrath of the cane. I only wanted to live in peace, and they took that away from me, with their painted faces and ugly sneers. I only wanted the warmth of a mother's touch, and yet all I get is a cold blow. It is tiring to be kind all the time, to smile as if my body doesn't ache with bruises and a shattered heart. Why can't I feel the hatred that boils my blood, feel the smirk that threatens to mar my face? It would be so easy to let go, to throw the cinders into their face, laugh as it blinds them, turning their face into a shade of black that matches their heart. And yet, you stay me, with your wraith-like hands and haunted voice. You tell me that everything will be alright, that magic will set me free. I laugh at you, ha! There is no such thing as fairy godmothers or golden pumpkin carriages, only pain and suffering. But no more. I will fight back, I will not be a damsel. I will become a harpy and rain fury and blood on those who seek to destroy me. I am ashes in your eyes; small and grey, but I will smother you.

Wolf-blood

They call me little girl, sweet child, but I raise my hackles against such saccharine words. I am not sugar-sweet, or as innocent as they believe me to be. I hunger and thirst for things my mother would admonish me for if she knew my inner thoughts. I want blood pumping in my veins, my heart accelerating with adrenaline, with zest. I want and I need. But they only pat me on the head like a dog and tell me to be obedient. Don't talk to strangers, my mother says, stay on the path, she warns me. I growl at her with bared teeth in answer. Let me go! I want to howl at her. Let me be free! The forest calls to me, like a siren song, and I need to answer it. I want to run through the trees, wind in my face and tangling my fur until it becomes a knotted mess that no brush can undo. I want mud on my legs as I wade through murky waters, want it to absorb into my skin until I am dirty all over and not even the clearest lake could cleanse me. The forest is my home, and I need to leave. I need to find my pack; it's not here in this small town that aims to dress me up in frilly clothes and tell me what is right and wrong, this place with ignorant people who don't yearn for something greater, for something more. And I want more. I want freedom, adventure, life, excitement. I want to feel my breath leaving my chest, want to feel the harsh bark beneath my fingers. Why must I listen to my mother? She doesn't listen to me, doesn't hear my wants. All she sees is an angel that must be cherished, a placid doll that must be dressed and strangled in the name of protection. Doesn't she see that I am no maiden with rosy cheeks? The only rose is the red of my hot blood wailing for release, like the sharp cry of a harpy. Doesn't she know I carry wolf-blood in me, that I long to howl at the moon and stars and run? Take me, forest, for I am yours.

Hypnos

I am asleep, yet I hear everything. I hear the sounds of snoring reverberating throughout the castle, hear the bramble and vines twisting over cold stone. I am asleep and awake at the same time, caught in between life and death. Oh, how foolish was I to be tricked by a needle! Was that some forgotten gift bestowed upon me, to be thoughtless and irrational? Did my parents only wish for me to be beautiful for my husband, to be seen and not heard, to not have my own thoughts? Was that what they hoped when they gazed on me, did they see me as something to be bartered? If only I could escape this curse! I can feel time passing, and yet I stay the same. Was that another wish of my parents? That I would stay young and beautiful so that it would be easy for me to ensnare the next handsome man? I wish I could escape from this infernal chain, run from this place and be free, but I can't escape. I can't escape him as he climbs up the stairwell, sword glinting in the candlelight, shoulders and back straight with determination. I can hear his sure footsteps as he stalks towards my bed, hear his breath hitch as he looks upon me. I wish I could sneer at him, mutilate my pretty visage so

he could run from me in terror. But I am
immobile, unable to flinch as he touches my face
and slips his fingers down my dress, molesting
my skin. I try to move, to scream, anything to
stop him, but he crawls over me, clutching at me
with greedy hands. Was this what my parents
wanted for me?

Queen of Beauty

They proclaimed me the most beautiful woman in the world, but I didn't want the title. Don't they see the woman behind the body? Don't they know that I am more than hips to bear children, full lips to kiss until they bleed red? All my life I have been lusted over, a prize to be possessed by greedy hands who only know how to tarnish and maim. Then you came, a king among men, and for the first time, I believed I was safe. Only the Fates brought him in the night, an Adonis who prowled towards me, stalking me. He pillaged and plundered, until I lay boneless, soul and body scarred and beaten. We disappeared, he with his prize, me wrapped in golden chains. I was presented like a prized bull and they saw my beauty, but nothing more. I raged inside, lightning in my veins that ached to strike down, but I wasn't divine like my father. I was a caged bird, compelled to sing whenever he wished. Then came the thousand ships and salvation. But blinded as I was, I didn't see the destruction, the giant horse that spelled death. I didn't foresee the walls crumbling like broken clay, the spears that would pierce young and old flesh. I can still hear the screaming, the smell of blood as carrion birds descended onto bodies, beaks ripping into dead skin. I can feel them clasping at me from the pits of Tartarus, trying to drag me to the depths. Where did I go wrong? I plead with them. I cry as I beat my breast with hatred and despair. Damn this wretched body, the voluptuous skin that men worship instead of a sacred shrine. Maybe if I was born a man, I would've freed myself from this wretched life. But that is the price of beauty's curse.

A Rose by Another Name

I am the treasured daughter of a noble family, sweet and chaste. I am just and pure, but you don't see the chains shackling me. A pretty canary, he says. You must sing and dance for the people, you must woo them until they fall at your feet. A gilded cage for a gilded bird. Doesn't he know that I yearn to soar above the clouds, that my desires are loftier than his? I am more than an offspring of his name, another branch to this great tree of lineage. I am more than a brood-mare at an auction house, waiting to be sold to the highest bidder. And then I met you – my violent delight. With one holy palmer's kiss, you opened the cage. Ready was I to roam free, too late did I realise that you were another captor. I was just another Rosalind to you, some otherworldly pillar of piety and beauty that the great bards spoke of. Through Cupid's eyes you didn't see my doubts, my fears – only a coveted rose that you plucked out of the garden. You bound me to you, until all I could do was breathe you. Not even death could separate us, the dagger a pinprick against my breast. I will never be known as my own, only as your Juliet.

Call of the Wild

They call me Beauty, for that is what I am. Beautiful smile, beautiful hair, beauty, beauty, beauty! Bah, what wasteful words! Beauty is a fleeting notion – here one moment, then poof! Gone. Don't they know that deep inside lies a hunger, ready to unleash itself on the world? Beneath this veneer is an ugliness that yearns to make an appearance. Oh, how they would quiver in horror to see their darling Beauty roar with a vengeance. They think I'm a simple village girl, waiting and wanting to be married, to be a mother and a good wife. But I am so much more than these provincial fantasies. I am more creature than woman, hunting down the fools who think they can mark me with their false compliments. They are my prey; I am the predator. I take and take and take until I am satiated. I have more heart and more spirit, a member of Artemis' band of wild companions. No one can conquer me. If they try, beware my fangs and claws for they are sharp and will cut you down like a sword. There is a beast lying in wait inside this beauty – wait until she thunders.

Rue

I was the white carnation and daisy in a garden of thorns and thickets. I bloomed only for you, my sad-eyed and doleful prince. They told me that your heart did not belong to me, but I did not listen. My clove heart was yours from the moment your words, words, words pulled me into your orbit. I was the moon to your sun, yearning to touch you for one small moment. Your lips stroked my skin until it blushed like a red rose. I fell into your arms, and I blossomed, a woman renewed. What lies you spoke of, with those black dahlia lips! With a hateful look, you pushed me away. Get thee to a nunnery! Brief, thy name is woman's love! I do not understand, this feeling of joy and grief intermingling with the other. It consumes and buries me like the soil over the grave. Such words pierce the soul and cloud the mind. What do you know of my love? It is as constant and pure as the rose, but you turned it into a weed. Pluck it out, pluck pluck pluck! Black rose and fungus for you, rue and purple hyacinth for me. Now my garden is dry and withered – let me water it in the lake yonder.

Le Morte d'amour

They call me the downfall of your kingdom, but they don't know that I bled for it as well. They call me whore, betrayer of kings, but they don't know that you betrayed me, your queen. In times gone by, I did love you, the champion of the world. You with your mighty sword – a sight to behold. I was swept away by the courtly dances, kisses bestowed on hands. My favour was wrapped around your wrist, so that all in the land would know that we were one. But then you were pulled in by seductive eyes and a lascivious smile. You say you were compelled by outside forces, but your eyes could not lie. They told me of stolen moments, of bodies entwining together. I then took my revenge on you. With the rage of Hera scorned by her deceitful husband, I sought comfort in the arms of my knight, my hero. Like the flash of a supernova, our bodies and souls consumed the other. He loved me with righteous passion, and I fell. Fell in love, out of love - such warring emotions affect the soul! But happiness does not last for sinners like us. You, slain at the battlefield, and I, hidden away from the earthly

world. If we had listened to your mage's
prophecy, would we have escaped the wheel of
fate?

Pomegranate

They think I'm the prettiest flower in the garden,
meek and virgin-like. But they don't know that
behind cornflower-blue eyes, my heart is bleak
as ash and strong as steel. They see me as a
precious gem that must be secreted away from
lustful eyes, wandering hands that seek to crush
my daffodil hair and white rose body. But don't
they know that I have thorns that prick, teeth
that bite? Doesn't she see that I'm withering
underneath her green thumb, rotting like dead
flowers, only she keeps me while she prunes
them away, those lucky dead blooms. Death was
far from reach, that beautiful black hole of
oblivion, until you came on the wings of a bat.
You were a stain on Eden's garden, yet my
deadness spoke to yours, souls finding each
other. People say you spirited me away, but they
don't know that I lunged for you, hands gripping
darkness as I whispered in your ear, 'Take me
away, husband.' You wrapped me in your cloak
of death, and it felt like the softest of petals was
brushing against my skin. And then we
disappeared in a cloud of shadow to arrive in
your domain of eternal night and cold, and I
knew I was home. People say I was tricked to

eat the blood-seeds, but they don't know that I came up with the idea, eager I was to stay with you, my lord of the dead. They tasted like sin, like molten gold and I felt the juice dripping down my chin, staining my lips red. I kissed you then, bloody lips upon ghost-white, and when you smiled at me with red in your teeth, I knew you were mine. But spring came for me, the blades of grass pulling me back towards the earth, away from you, my love. They are glad to see me safe amongst the fields and blossoms, but they don't see the six dark seeds I hide. They took me away, thinking they had won, but don't they know that they can't beat Lady Death?

Part 2: The Condemned

Wicked

They say I am evil, a jealous beauty with a black heart, ready to kill any rival. And so I am, but I wasn't always like this. I used to be kind and gentle, with a cherubic smile on my face. I was too innocent to know the ways of the world. They told me not to run off with you, you with the wide grin and eyes that told of adventure and mischief. But I didn't listen, only the rush of my heart beating as you kissed me with strong lips could be heard. I was in love, and you loved me too. I gave you myself, you took with laughter and hands that sizzled my skin. We spent three nights together, and then you had to leave. You said you would find your fortune and you would come back for me. I waited and waited, my heart and stomach full of love. But you never came back, lost in another woman's pretty mouth and eyes. They called me foolish, lustful, too stupid to know that I was only a passing fancy. Nine months of despair, I lost love again, ripped from my hands to become Death's child. You took my heart, so I took yours with a knife. Red like love, red like blood. I was surrounded in it, with no hope to escape. So I gladly drank it, encasing myself in steel and darkness, smiling with a devil's smile as men fell to their knees before me, fear and wonder in their eyes. Long live the wicked.

Chicken Feet

They call me a hag, witch, devil-spawn with iron teeth and flame eyes, but they only say that because they are scared of me. Of my power, that burns and boils until there is nothing left but the hot, wild energy that flows through my veins. I used to be the wise woman that people would come to for aid, to soothe their broken limbs and calm their troubled minds. I would help children with their letters and numbers and assist in childbirth. I was the matchmaker, the healer, the mother. But they soon began to be fearful of me. They couldn't control that which cannot be tamed. They drew back from me, spitting on me with disgust and hatred, flinging insults that would mar my back as I would walk in the village. She deals with black magic, they would whisper as I gathered herbs during the witching hour, talk in strange tongues as I made salves and pastes for the sick. For one so ugly could only deal with dark power. Don't they know I did this out of love for them? That I would do so gladly, if it meant that the children and mothers and orphans and maidens would be safe? But they cast me out like a leper, beating me until I could no longer walk and blood dripped onto the ground like my tears. But I knew no one could protect like I could, for I have no restrictions, no limitations. Nothing could stop me, not even the tsar. And so I crawled to the forest, the voices in the leaves murmuring reassurances to me, guiding me to the clearing where I would set up my house with the chicken feet and smoking chimney. And there I was free, like the wind and the sea, free to concoct and plan and wait. Wait until fair maidens with troubled lives would come knocking on my door, in search of wisdom, knowledge and truth. And I would say:

Why have you come to Baba Yaga?

Fathoms Below

I fell for you, my jolly sailor bold. I shackled myself to you, and you did the same, or so I thought. We tied ourselves to each other, and I felt as if I had found my reason. We spent countless days on the beach, skin kissing skin, until you eclipsed everything in my sight. I told you secrets, of the magic in my veins, scared that you would hate me, but you didn't, did you? You said I was precious, a treasure that should be protected. You were so gentle to me, like a mother with her child. I felt safe with you, my sailor, that I gave you my heart and soul. I knew you would never forsake me. Such a foolish thought, for how could I know that you had the key with you the whole time? Where I was bound, you were able to free yourself and then they came for me. Witch, they exclaimed with pitchforks and torches. I knew you betrayed me. My heart started to crumble like ash, but the water saved me. She called for me. Lorelei. Lorelei. She called, and I answered with a scream. The water became me, and I became the water, a tempestuous force that could not be diminished, no chain could bind me, and I felt liberated. Do you hear my scream as you sail

away on your ship, do you feel your blood
cooling as my voice caresses your skin? Hear
me, come to me, and we can be one again. Walk
the plank, my sailor, stretch out your hand. I'm
reaching for you with claws for hands, fangs for
teeth, but all you see is the fair maiden with the
gold hair and sapphire eyes. Listen to my song
as I kiss you and pull you under, listen to the
thrumming of your heart, the clenching of your
lungs as it fights for one more gasp of air, the
water that lulls you to an eternal sleep. Listen to
my siren song, binding you once more to me and
my rock.

Snake Eyes

I once was a beautiful maiden, with flowing hair and a face radiant as the sun. Men would flock to me, waxing poetic and making promises of love, but I turned away from them. My virtue and loyalty to the gods were more sacred to me than the lies coming out from a man who would let his eyes and hands wander. I stayed pure as a newborn babe, my soul as clear as the glistening waves of the sea. But oh, how turbulent are those waters! They surrounded me, dragging me away from the temple of divine holiness that was my home and plunged me into darkness. The sea filled me until I became part of it, of him. I cried, begged for your help, sure that you would see that I was not to blame for such defilement, sure that you would aid in my escape. But you turned your back on me, disgust and anger causing your heavenly face to turn ugly, and that's what you made me. You took my lovely hair and turned it into a nest of snakes slithering over my cheeks, whispering to me to that it was my fault, my sin to bear. My soulful gaze you turned deadly, my body a monstrous beast that would only bear other monsters. I wanted to scream my innocence, but you abandoned me, my saviour, discarding me to the world of men. Fine, let it be so. I will abandon you and your false teachings of righteousness, for how it can it be righteous to punish the victim? You made me into a terror, and so I will become one. Watch your creation at work, o false-benevolent one, watch as she devours any man who crosses her path, taking her revenge into her talons. Be wary of me, wandering soul, for I will turn you until your heart becomes stone-cold. Just like me.

Swan Song

They call me your twin, your evil doppelganger that caused you to suffer at the hand of my owl-father. I am your shadow that walks your every move. I am your voice, your smile, but inside I am screaming. Don't they know that I was a puppet on a string, made to dance, to laugh, to whisper seductive words into your prince's ear? But I was made the fool, for just a wrinkle in time, I believed in that fantasy. I was the one who was loved by many, who would dance under the moonlight with my love until the dawn turned my rosy skin into glistening white feathers. What a cruel fate you lived, my swan-sister, but what passion you endured! I didn't know black meant desolation and constriction until I danced with him through your eyes. I wanted to consume your pain, your joy until it entwined with my soul, until it became mine. I yearn for what you feel, to rip myself from your shackles and make my name my own, to be my own. Don't I deserve the same things as you, sweet sister? Aren't I more than a dark reflection of you? I have my desires, my wants, but they are just ripples in a lake, small and fleeting. Wishes are not meant for an ugly duckling who will never grow into a swan.

Bloody Dagger

I was a poor nobleman's daughter when I first met you on your white steed, your armour flashing in the sun like a piece of gold. I knew you were the one for me, for only you could sate my thirst for more, to change my dirt-stained clothes for swathes of silk and satin. We were twin flames, bound to burn the world around us in our ferocity, until all that was left to burn was ourselves. Oh, how I wish the weird sisters spoke to me in their riddles, forewarning me of my doom! Out, damned ambition, out I say! Let me wash myself of this vaulting feeling, let me clean myself of you and your lack of inaction. My only sin was to love you, to be your rock when you stumbled in your doubts of hesitation. I let the spirits unsex me so that we could succeed where you failed. I became the serpent under the flower, squirming into your ear, purring words to inspire you, to move you to act with voracious hunger. I took upon the dagger in your name, let the blood taint my hands. Nevermore will they be clean, never be sweetened by the perfumes of Arabia. I did it all for you, husband mine, death and eternal

damnation my reward. Then this I make to you,
a blood promise sealed with a kiss – let our souls
dance in the fiery depths, always burning,
always bleeding.

Dragon Wings

They say fairies are the epitome of grace, but they never met me. Bat wings, night-sky eyes, and skin the colour of jade, I was an outcast to my fellow kin. Don't they know there is beauty in darkness? For without night, there could be no day. But all they could see was an abomination. Monster. Demon. All I wanted was someone to love me. Then you three came along, with your bursts of light and goodness. Flora, Fauna, Merryweather – even your names were rays of sunshine that enveloped me in eternal brightness. You took me in, I became a sister and found a home. But even the purest of hearts can turn black with disdain. My darkness became too much for your light, too overpowering. You saw something that needed containment, not love. I was a pet to you, an unruly animal that couldn't be tamed. Like rags, I was discarded, too dirty to taint those godly-clean hands of yours. You gave me hope only to take it from me. Now you have set your eyes on one younger, more malleable. A red rose whose thorns you are ready to pluck. But be wary sisters, I am never far behind. I will be the

dragon in this story you desperately try to write,
ready to rage hellfire on your precious dawn.

House of Sweets

A woman lives for her children, they say. I did
not understand until I felt your heartbeat-feet at
my stomach, making your presence known. You
were my salvation in my world of loneliness.
Two sunbeams running through the forest,
laughter joining the birdsong, faces stained from
the muddy banks you played in. I had created
our sweet-house as a token of our joy, and your
chipmunk-cheeks would bulge while devouring
my love for you. But then the darkness shrouded
your light, taking you away from me. Where did
you go, my turtledoves? Don't go where I can't
follow. Despair and desolation replaced love and
bliss, encroaching me until I was choking on it.
A black hole became my heart, pumping grief
and pain instead of blood. Come back to me,
sweet ones, come back to your mother's arms.
Your house of sweets is waiting for you, with its
iced roof and cookie door. Hark – is that them I
hear? They're calling for me. Mother, we are
here! I see them through the sugar-frosted
windows, grubby knees and twigs caught in hair.
My children! I've been waiting for you. Come,
let us sit by the fire. You must be hungry, you're
skin and bones! Come, let your mother feed you

until you become nice and plump. I will never let you go, my sweetlings. Mother has missed you.